LIGHT AT HAND

Light at Hand

PHOTOGRAPHS
1970–85

Guy Mendes

FOREWORD BY ED MCCLANAHAN
AFTERWORD BY JONATHAN WILLIAMS

GNOMON PRESS

Frontispiece:
On Lake Pontchartrain, Louisiana, 1975

Copyright © 1986 by Guy Mendes

ISBN 0-917788-30-3

LC Catalog Card Number 85-81724

Thanks to the Kentucky Arts Council,
the National Endowment for the Arts,
and the Frankfort Arts Foundation,
for making publication of this book
possible. Jonathan Williams' *Afterword*
first appeared in *Conjunctions* and
thanks are due to Bradford Morrow
for permission to reprint it here.

Published by Gnomon Press,
P.O. Box 106, Frankfort,
Kentucky 40602-0106

FOREWORD

"If I hadn't believed it, I wouldn't have seen it."
—attributed to Armadillo, a hippie of the Sixties

WHEN GUY MENDES TOOK THE PICTURE of Little Enis, "The World's Greatest Left-Handed Upside-down Guitar Player," and the girls! girls! girls! on the sidewalk in front of Boot's Bar (a drinking resort located in the old Scott Hotel at the corner of Scott Street and South Broadway in Lexington, Kentucky—"the beautiful Hotel Scott Hilton," Enis used to say, "overlookin' the Southern Railroad tracks"), Guy stood in the gutter with his camera, and I stood in the street just behind him, directing traffic, endeavoring to prevent Guy from getting himself squashed by some wayward ogler at the wheel.

It was 1972, late afternoon on an April weekday, quittin' time in a workingman's neighborhood, and the sudden manifestation on the street corner of seven ladies in a virtual state of nature, however dubious their charms, was enlivening the usually desultory South Broadway swing-shift traffic jam. Horns were blaring, brakes were squealing, the air was rent by wolf whistles, hootings and hollerings, shouted avowals of eternal love, rash assertions of manly vigor and stamina, unorthodox propositions and unseemly imprecations. "Hey buddy," a wit in a pickup yelled at the intrepid boy photographer, "I see yer Brownie!" There was even a fender-bender in the intersection, and, adding a rhythm section to the cacaphony, a freight train rattling through.

But photographers are a single-minded lot; show 'em the real world, and what do they see? A *picture* of it! (As a writer, naturally, I hold to the view that the world is made not of pictures, but of words.) So, precisely at the epicenter of this scene of tumult and clamor, there occurs the sly wink of the camera's shutter, and—*click!*—the human race has a striking new portrait of itself, a study in the mortality of the flesh and the valor of the spirit, funny yet poignant, affectionate yet unsentimental . . . Well, turn to that photograph in these pages and see for yourself. This time the picture wins, hands down.

I have pulled some duty, friends, in the excellent company of Guy Mendes, both behind his camera and in front of it. We've been pals and running-mates since the early 1970s, when I spent a year in Lexington, teaching at the University of Kentucky and writing what turned out to be an article about Little Enis for *Playboy* magazine, and Guy was on the scene as a guiding light of *the blue-tail fly,* one of the brightest, sassiest, most audacious underground newspapers in the country. Guy was also beginning to get serious about photography, and together we logged a lot of hours hanging out with Enis, who turned out to be a rich subject for both of us.

(*Playboy* used Guy's photograph of Enis and the Enisettes to illustrate the article, but, being *Playboy,* they couldn't resist tarting it up with a mishmash of trashy "artwork." Fine to see it here in all its naked splendor.)

As it happened, I was a pretty fair subject myself, that year. "Hey, you were in costume!" exclaimed a friend the other day when I showed him the picture of me that graces this book. Well, yes, I admitted, I was—but in 1972 I wore that costume *all the time,* see, I mean that's who I was *being* then, that sike-o-deelic refugee from a Smirnoff ad. Guy swears he positioned the light behind my Ed the Terrible headpiece merely to suggest that I had an aura all my own, and steadfastly disavows any intention of hinting at the holes I sported in my head in those days. Anyhow, I love the picture; it reminds me of someone I once knew.

In fact, I love *all* these pictures. The camera has the reputation of being a cold, objective instrument, but Guy Mendes' portraits are unfailingly warm, good humored, even playful. His landscapes are serene and spacious, his studies of the textures of light and shadow are adventurously abstract and "painterly," his interiors and still lifes are elegantly composed. There's an abundant variety of things to look at in this book: from a *trompe l'oeil* toad to a famous poet to a Hudson River School landscape to a graceful torso to a crumbling Grecian portico that seems somehow to metamorphose into a tattered fragment of sheet music . . . Vision, Swift tells us, is the art of seeing the invisible. Guy Mendes sees it every time—and takes its picture.

The old Chinese proverb had the right score all along: Pictures 1000, Words 1.

ED MCCLANAHAN

1. Home, Cow & Country, 1978

2. Irises, 1978

3. Cow Rags, Jessamine County, 1975

4. Wendell Berry, Henry County, 1970

5. Harlan Hubbard on the Ohio River, 1982

6. Glendolough Monastery, Ireland, 1981

7. The River Dee, Dentdale, England, 1981

8. Buzzards' Roost, Woodford County, 1980

9. Kentucky Ernie Ford, Franklin County, 1978

10. Leonard Webb, Macon County, North Carolina, 1975

11. Jonathan Williams, Gatlinburg, 1974

12. Edgar Tolson, Campton, 1974

13. Lily in the Bathroom, 1983

14. Dogwood, Red River Gorge, 1985

15. Howard Finster at his World Folk Art Church, Inc., Georgia, 1984

16. St. EOM, a.k.a. Eddie Owens Martin, in his "Land of Pasaquan," Georgia, 1984

17. Captain Kentucky, a.k.a. Ed McClanahan, 1972

18. Harry Furnival, Woodchester, England, 1981

19. Janice and Teri, 1973

20. The Baths, Virgin Gorda, British Virgin Islands, 1983

21. Torso, 1980

22. Cave on Marble Creek, Jessamine County, 1980

23. Bow of the "Island Fever," British Virgin Islands, 1981

24. Carnegie Cars, Cumberland Island, Georgia, 1975

25. Plum Orchard, Cumberland Island, Georgia, 1978

26. Hartford Railroad Station, Connecticut, 1972

27. Dungeness Poolhouse, Cumberland Island, Georgia, 1974

28. Toad, Gifford Island, Nova Scotia, 1980

29. Long Island Pond, 1984

30. Guy Davenport, Lexington, 1975

31. Robert Tharsing, 1974

32. Bamboo Avenue, Jamaica, 1980

33. Torso, 1978

34. Palmetto, Cumberland Island, Georgia, 1973

35. Chard, 1975

36. Up on Eleanor, 1979

37. Ben, Berks County, Pennsylvania, 1972

38. Charlie Yellow Calf and Darrell Rice, 1978

39. Paul Metcalf, Berkshire County, Massachusetts, 1975

40. The Fabulous Little Enis and the Go-Go Girls of Boot's Bar, Lexington, 1972

41. Ramsey McLean at the Fauborg, New Orleans, 1983

42. Sister Gertrude Morgan in her Everlasting Gospel Revelation Mission, New Orleans, 1974

43. Ralph Eugene Meatyard, 1970

44. Mémé, 1982

45. Eleanor Out Back, 1978

AFTERWORD

The Photographs of Guy Mendes:
"Eh, La Bas, the F-Stops Here!"

GORE VIDAL WENT TO SEE E.M. Forster on some occasion back in the 1960s in his rooms at King's College, Cambridge. And the old man revealed the existence of his proto-gay novel, *Maurice,* which has male characters in bed, etc. "And what did they do?" asked Mr. Vidal, the ever-practical, inquisitive, politely lascivious American. "Talk," muttered the Englishman.

When it comes to "photographic talk," it can usually be guaranteed to bore the tits off a hog, to use the vernacular of Woodford County, Kentucky, where Mr. Guy Marius Mendes, III lives in meta-hick repose. In fact, I am almost reduced to silence by a sentence from the venerable Ralph Steiner: "No word person writing on photography has ever said anything that helped me do better on Thursday what I'd done less well on Wednesday."

But my intention is otherwise. First, to give you the merest sketch of this amiable and attractive *boulevardier* and *bricoleur* from the City of New Orleans, who has settled down in the Blue Grass with a cow or two and a mule and some old dawgs in a cabin dating back to the 18th century. Just recently it has been instructive to see the photographer here in the new landscape of the Cumbrian dales, nicely kitted out in corduroy knickerbockers and revolutionist's cap from the days of Tatlin, as he shifted his view-camera about in the rain, pointing it at the fells, at the dry river bed of Easegill, at the stone circle of Castle Rigg, and at the bales of plastic-wrapped hay below the Stennerskeugh Clouds. There is more than a touch of Monsieur Hulot about G. Mendes as he goes about his playful business, and Lartigue may well be a cousin on the distaff side. And then I get a slight *frisson*—a combination Deputy Dawg and debonair wire-haired vyzsla (that exotic breed only available from the writer Charles Newman at his "Hungry Mother Kennels" at Volney, near Mouth of Wilson in the Virginia Blue Ridge).

A few quick questions, to help flesh out the gentleman:

JONATHAN WILLIAMS: Why did you set up as a photographer and take pictures?

GUY MENDES: Because it feels good. As the great lady, Aretha Franklin, says: "DON'T SEND ME NO DOCTOR." The doctor is already "in." That is, there's a bit of the doctor in each of us. Which is to say: SOOTH YOURSELF! Also, perhaps you do it to SUIT YOURSELF. You suit yourself first. Suppose you iron a cotton shirt and put it on. It might make you look nice in public, but really, it's how it feels across your back. How it feels to you is the important thing—if you're a cotton lover. Suiting yourself is not necessarily a selfish way of going at it. What you are trying to do is surprise yourself with the light, to remind yourself of delight. If you can do it for yourself, maybe you can make delight tangible for others too.

Another reason I photograph is that my mother had such good ears. From early childhood she could hear a piece of music once and sit down and play it on the piano. She could really "radiate the 88's," as they say down in New Orleans. In her middle years, my mother began to study and practice classical piano works. It was her therapy, both mental and physical (for arthritis of the hands). It was also her delight. It was for her a way to let the heart out. She never performed professionally, but for years she played free for nursing homes, mental hospitals, church groups, alcohol rehab centers, and so on. One of her most popular numbers was an Old Mardi Gras tune, "If Ever I Cease To Love." . . . On the other hand, I'm lucky I can play the radio. If I could, I'd play the piano like Professor Longhair, or the sax like Earl Turbington, two New Orleans greats. But I didn't inherit my mother's ears. So I thought I'd try the eyes. To let the light in, to let the heart out. Maybe they can help me feel like Clifton Chenier, the Cajun accordionist, when he says, "I feel like a jet!"

JW: What do you take pictures of?

GM: Whatever gets in the way, whenever I have the time and patience and presence of mind to see it. By "things that get in the way," I don't mean the usual obstructions and diversions which claim our attention in the make-enough/get-enough world. I'm not talking about high dis-interest rates or the price of jeans. A photographer needs to be in a state of relaxed attention, call it, in order to stumble one way or another into a new place. Sometimes our response to the play of light is like the response of the unsuspecting student, who, while trying hard to medi-tate, is suddenly, without warning, whacked across the back with a two by four by the Zen Master. The Master is trying to elicit a kind of sur-prise satori—or at least wake up a sleepy student. When light falls in such spectacular manner that we can't fail to see it—as presence, as energy, as power—it's like being whacked across the back of the eyeballs. Wake up and take a look around! There is the line from a Roethke poem: "Light takes the tree, but who can tell us how?" Light takes the tree; and light takes me.

JW: You aren't one of those neo-regionalists, are you?

GM: No. But, if you are what you eat, it also holds that you are *where* you are. And where you've been. Where you are is what you see is what you get. I have lived mainly in two places: one in which people are ori-ented more towards water, and one in which people are oriented more towards land. It's not odd that I do waterscapes and landscapes. Place provides other influences too, such as music and food. The two halves of my brain are best characterized as the jazz/shrimp-fricasee side and the bluegrass/fried-chicken side. Part of me simmers in crab boil and another part bastes in eleven secret herbs and spices assembled by an old alchemist named Sanders from down around Corbin.

JW: Since you got the gift of gab (and a bucket of remoulade sauce to go with it), I ought to ask you to name ten favorite places, your ten favorite baroque composers and country fiddle players, your ten favorite foods or books or philosophers or structuralists or porn flicks. One wants to compare tastes and see how much smarter or dumber one is. Anyway, write down the names of photographers who abide with you, who you would hang on the wall, whose example rings clear. Give us a quick take on each.

GM: A shopping list of photographers I gradually got hold of after acquiring a camera in '68 is not hard to rattle off. But it leaves out the writers, painters and musicians who have had as much influence, or more. People like Wendell Berry and Ed McClanahan, Bob Tharsing and Ann Tower, Dr. John and the Neville Brothers can make even a slow-witted fellow like myself sit up and pay attention. The photographers who have had that effect on me include: Stieglitz, for his intensity, his missionary zeal; Edward Weston, who was equally single-minded, and whose veggies, nudes, and landscapes are touchstones for any student of the art; Walker Evans, Robert Frank and Lee Friedlander for showing us what was right under our noses all the time; Clarence John Laughlin, who has been pursuing houses and haunts (haints) for over half a century; J. H. Lartigue, a kid who taught us not to take ourselves so seriously; Minor White, who in spite of all his talk of making camerawork mystical, his pictures speak for themselves, thank you; and, finally, Gene Meatyard, whom I knew, and who taught me mainly that each of us, even opticians in suburban shopping centers, sees things differently; i.e., he looked normal, but he saw different.

JW: There's one word you do not use in noting the virtues and attributes of your photographers. And that is *form*. Charles Olson's line in *The Maximus Poems* continually sounds in my ear, like some great harp string: "ONE LOVES ONLY FORM . . ."

GM: Form and feeling seems to be what it's all about. Maybe it's the form that evokes the feeling. For instance, looking out of the window here at Corn Close, you see across the valley and up the next hill. The stone fences and hedgerows and tree lines that run across and up the long hill, the line of the hill top that bumps and rolls along against the sky, the white dots of sheep—all of those forms combine to convey feeling, the feeling of these parts. At one point on the horizontal line along the top of the hill/bottom of the sky, there is a break in a stone wall, a gap, an entrance, perhaps four feet wide. Through the gap, you see clouds. My eye is drawn to that opening in the wall. Even the gap is a form. But not every form fits in the black box. A *real* photograph—perhaps that's when you manage to get the form to fit in the box?

The prints in this book reveal a man with a particularly cordial and companionable imagination. The portraits, especially, indicate this. There are not many of us comfortable in the parlor of the learned Professor Davenport and equally at home with the likes of Campton's crafty carver of devil dolls, old Ed Tolson. Or with Kentucky Ernie Ford and Little Enis. I regret there is no image of Lexington, Kentucky's mysterious figure, Sweet Evening Breeze, who must have the prettiest name in the modern world . . . If we were talking about tennis, we'd say that GM plays with superb touch, without a lot of evident strain. Don't be put off by plain photographic pleasure. Such pleasure is rare and hardly frivolous or dumb in the head. As in the Creole word *lagniappe* (which you say lan-yap), Guy Mendes gives you "a little extra."

JONATHAN WILLIAMS

GNOMON PRESS
WOULD LIKE TO THANK THE FOLLOWING PATRONS
OF THIS BOOK FOR HELPING MAKE ITS
PRODUCTION POSSIBLE:

O. L. BUNN, INC.
JONATHAN GREENE
JAMES S. JAFFE
KENTUCKY ARTS COUNCIL
GUY M. MENDES, JR.

SPONSORS INCLUDE:

CHANDLER GORDON
JAMES BAKER HALL
BETTY ANN MEAD
MARTHA NELSON THOMAS
TERRY RUSSELL

This book has been set in Trump Mediaeval
by Graphic Composition, Inc. & printed
in 200 line duotone by Thomson-Shore,
Inc. in an edition of 2,000 copies.